To Jan Happy [...] from Nick -e

Holy Unacceptable

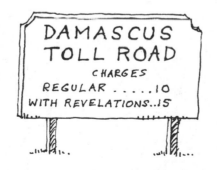

by the same author

A Hundred and One Uses of a Dead Cat
A Hundred and One More Uses of a Dead Cat
Unspeakable Acts
Odd Visions and Bizarre Sights
Stroked Through the Covers
Success and How To Be One
Teddy
Totally U.S.
Uniformity
Odd Dogs

Holy Unacceptable

SIMON BOND

Methuen

A Methuen Paperback

First published in Great Britain in 1990
by Methuen London
Michelin House, 81 Fulham Road, London SW3 6RB

Copyright © 1990 Polycarp Ltd
The author has asserted his moral rights

A CIP catalogue record is available for this book
from the British Library

ISBN 0 413 61970 2

Printed in England by Clays Ltd, St Ives plc

THE PURITANS ENJOY
A REAL GOOD LAUGH

ARCHBISHOP
THOMAS FLYNN
1890 – 1967

'ONE OF GOD'S
LITTLE HELPERS'

Joseph Smith Discovers Mormonism

A CONCISE MAP OF WORLD RELIGIONS

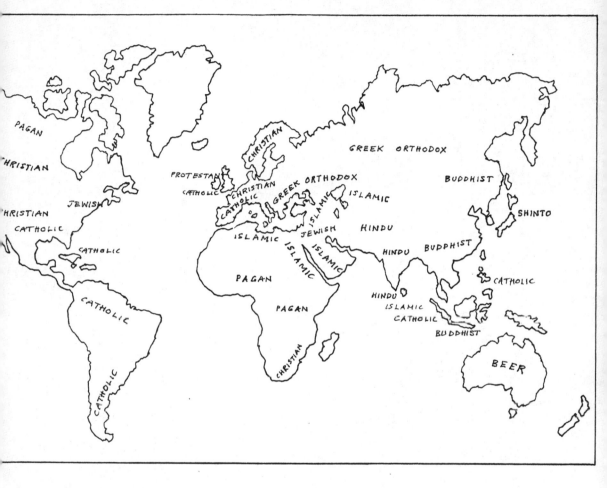

Saint Francis
changes his mind
about animals

HOW TO SPOT A CATHOLIC

THE SHROUD OF TURIN

(MARK 2)

5.40 PM ON THE SECOND DAY....
AND STILL WAITING FOR THE SURVEYOR

AND ON THE EIGHTH DAY
GOD HELD A SALE

HOW GOD INVENTED POLISH

'I just invented this...it's nice isn't it...I'm thinking of calling it a flower.'

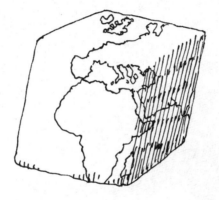

"Thou shalt not wear brown socks with black shoes."

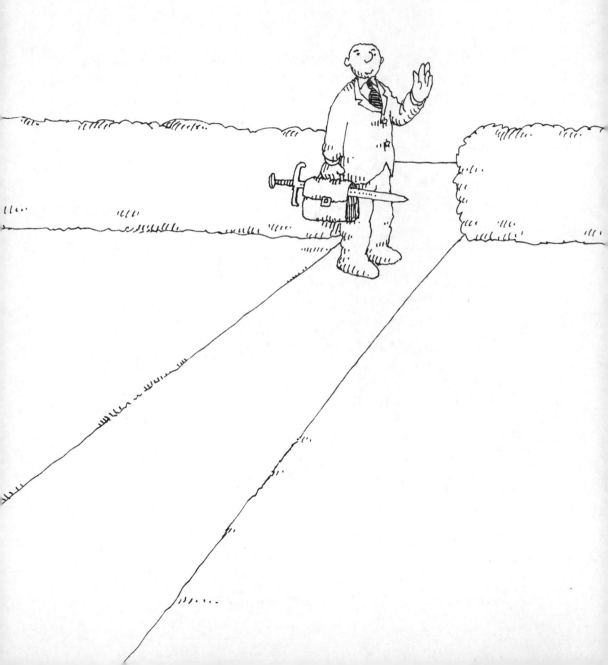

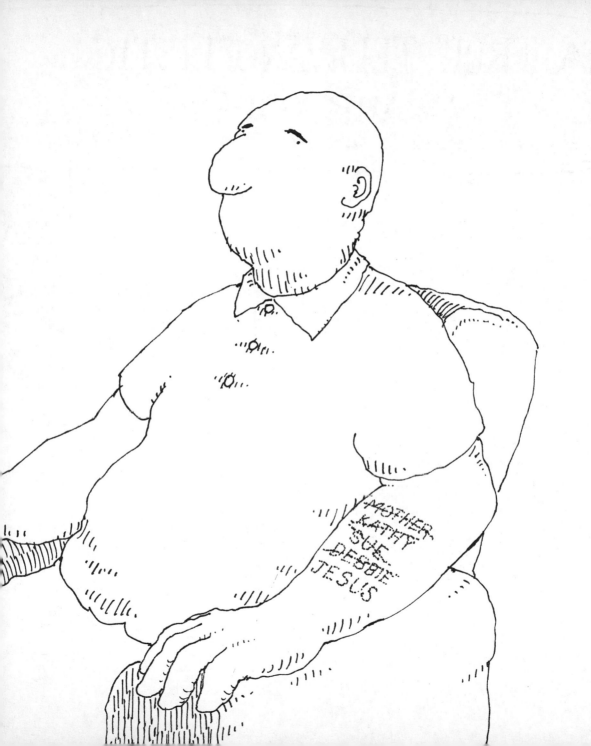

A TRUE TELEVANGELISTIC MIRACLE

MR & MRS ORTON BRIMBLES   PALULLA FALLS, TENN.   JULY 16TH 1974

WHY PEOPLE BECOME CHRISTIANS
(PROPORTIONAL DIAGRAM)

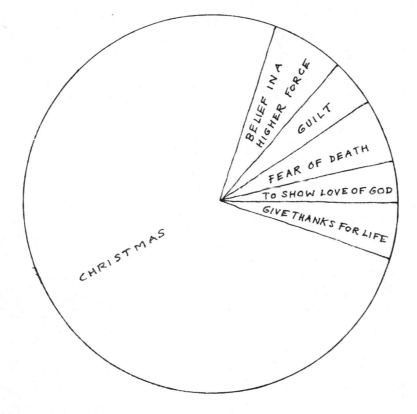

BELIEF IN A HIGHER FORCE

GUILT

FEAR OF DEATH

TO SHOW LOVE OF GOD

GIVE THANKS FOR LIFE

CHRISTMAS

'He used to be in advertising.'

MEMORABLE MIRACLES

BURNING BUSH

LOAVES & FISHES

WATER TO WINE

NON-STICK FRY PAN

LOW-CAL
ICECREAM

The Spanish Inquisition after a high wind.

'Thank you very much, it's all been very nice . . . well, except for the boiled fish.'

HARVEY KRISHNA
HARVEY KRISHNA

JEHOVAH

JEHOVAH'S
VICTIMS

JEHOVAH'S
WITNESSES

NOAH GETS OFF
TO A BAD START

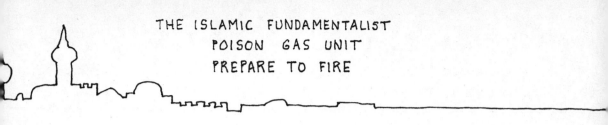

THE ISLAMIC FUNDAMENTALIST
POISON GAS UNIT
PREPARE TO FIRE

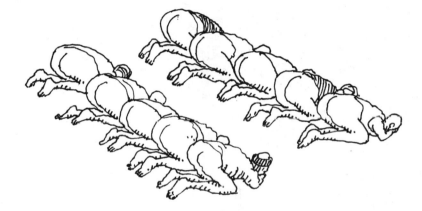

'Hey, this is a good bit – did I say that?'

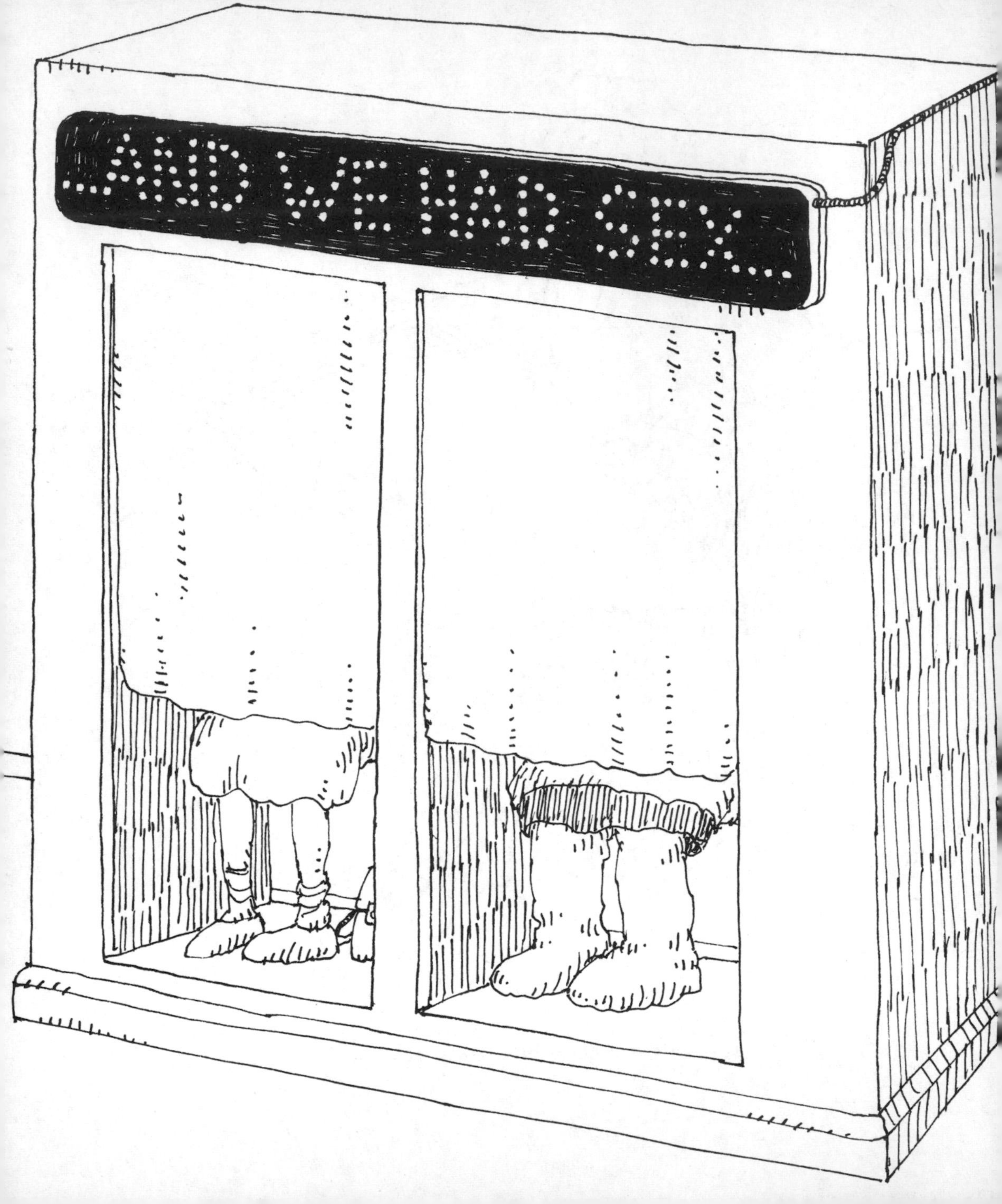
AND WE HAD SEX...

A HERETIC TURNED TO A STEAK

INFLATION HITS ST. THOMAS'S

WE NEED
~~25,000~~
~~25,000~~
48,000

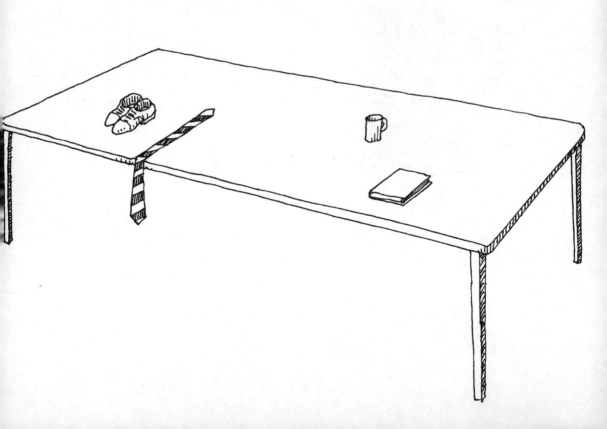

DAVID AND GOLIATH

'Last year
it was macramé,
this year
it's Christianity.'

The Stirrings of Liberalism

GOD SPEAKS TO REG DIBNER

MOSES IN THE BULLRUSHES

MOSES STILL IN THE BULLRUSHES

The Brothers of the Order of Saint Orson
Patron Saint of Fried Foods

Judas Iscariot makes
another 30 pieces of silver.

RELIGIOUS MYSTERIES No. 87

LIONEL (THE 13TH DISCIPLE?)

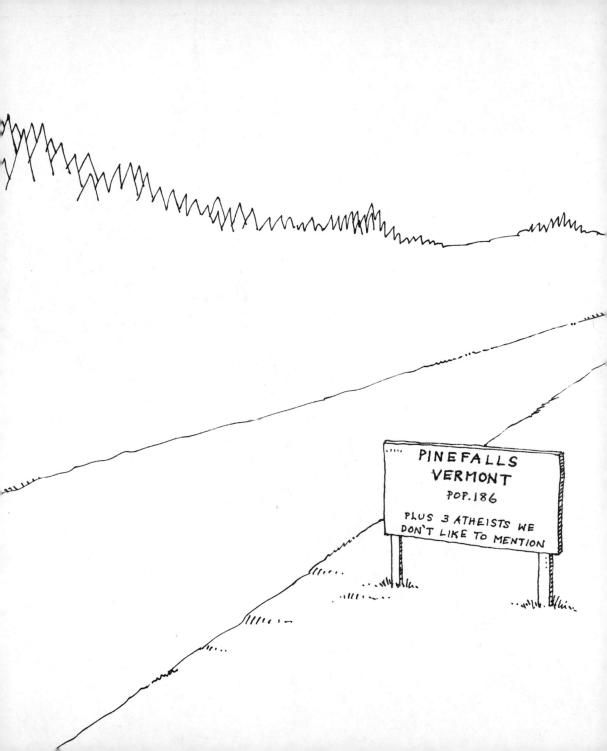

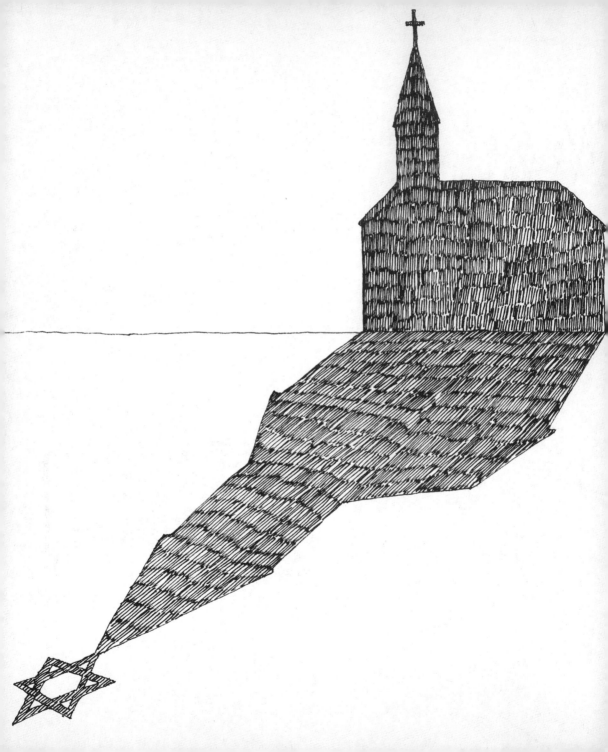

FUNDAMENTALIST MORMONS ATTACK A BOX OF TEA-BAGS

HE THREE WISE MEN
GUEST ON MIAMI VICE

'I'm your stand-in,
your Gideon Bible has been stolen.'

I'M SORRY I'M NOT HERE TO
ANSWER YOUR QUESTION...
IF YOU WOULD CARE TO LEAVE...

THE TEMPTATION OF CHRIST

JESUS SHOWS OFF A LITTLE BIT

Jesus gets flashy

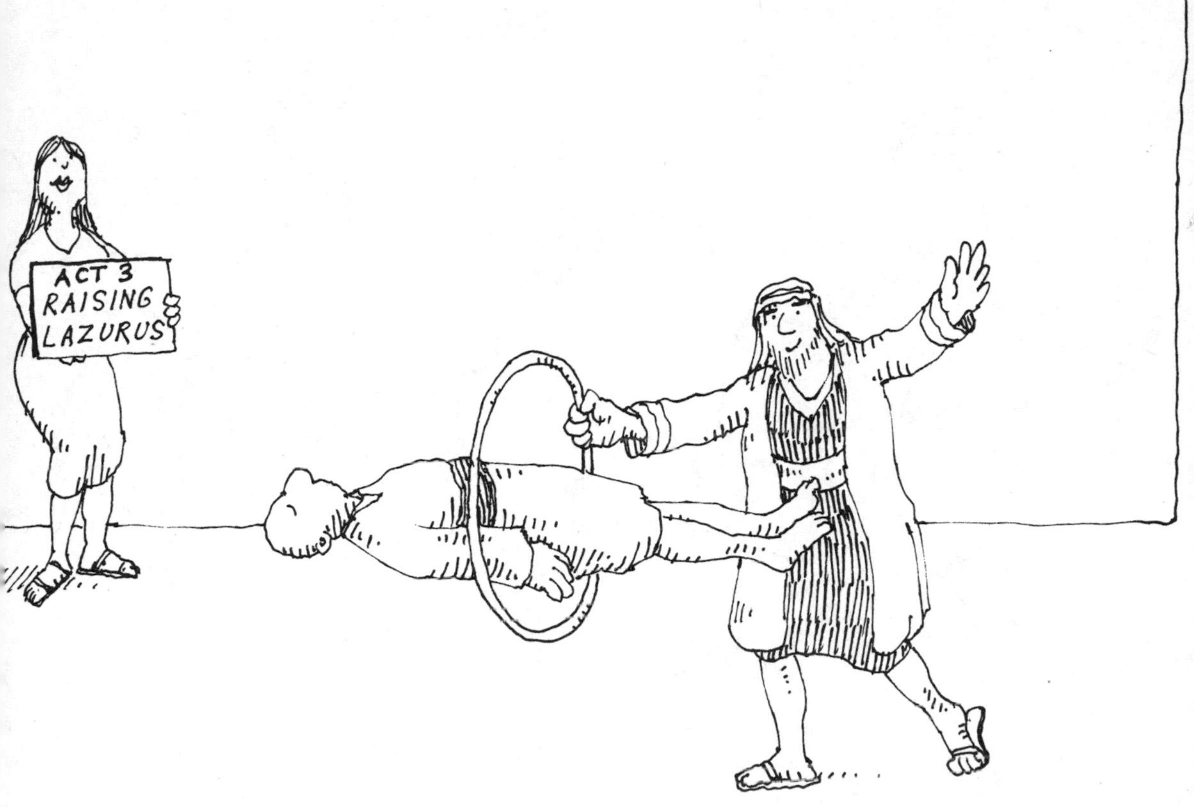

THE REAL REASON

AFTER THE LAST SUPPER

BORN-AGAIN BEES

A FUNDAMENTALIST BAPTIST CONVERTS A TOILET BOWL

THE POPE'S CHRISTMAS MESSAGE

THE BIZARRE CULT WORSHIP OF BOB HOPE

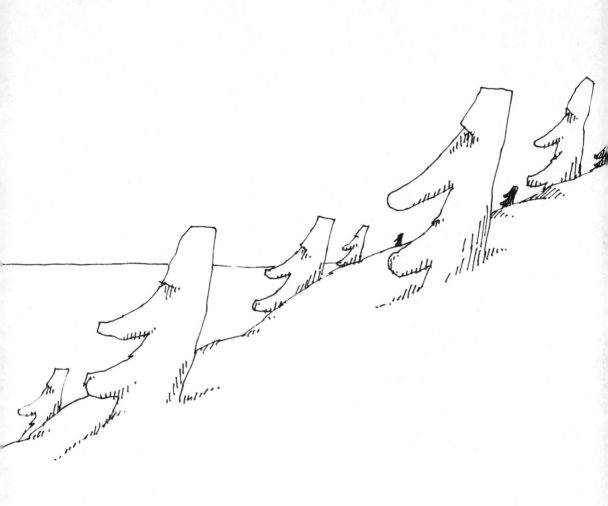

CYRANO DE BERGERAC
JOINS THE SPANISH INQUISITION

A RELIGIOUS ZEALOT DENOUNCES A TOASTER
FOR WORKING ON THE SABBATH.

THE ENDELL ST. BAPTIST CHURCH CHOIR'S
TRIP AROUND THE BAY COMES A CROPPER

LIFE DISAPPOINTS

AGAIN

'You're safe, he's still not coming.'